TABLE OF CONTENTS

T0020371

CHAPTER 1

BIG AND BLUE

Uranus is a big **planet**. It is the third largest planet in our **solar system**. Only Jupiter and Saturn are bigger. More than 60 Earths could fit inside!

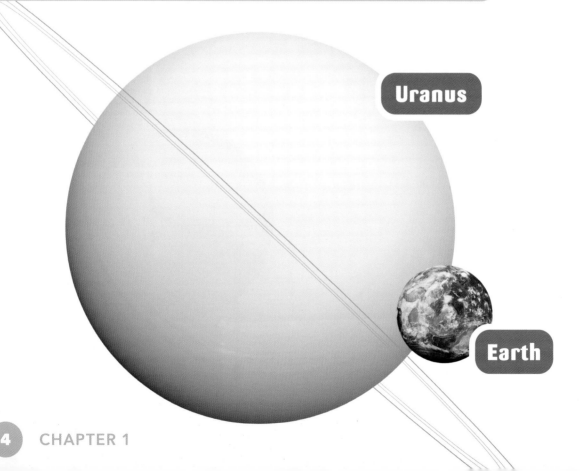

Uranus

Earth

OUR SOLAR SYSTEM
URANUS
THE COLDEST PLANET

by Mari Schuh

pogo

Ideas for Parents and Teachers

Pogo Books let children practice reading informational text while introducing them to nonfiction features such as headings, labels, sidebars, maps, and diagrams, as well as a table of contents, glossary, and index.

Carefully leveled text with a strong photo match offers early fluent readers the support they need to succeed.

Before Reading

- "Walk" through the book and point out the various nonfiction features. Ask the student what purpose each feature serves.
- Look at the glossary together. Read and discuss the words.

Read the Book

- Have the child read the book independently.
- Invite him or her to list questions that arise from reading.

After Reading

- Discuss the child's questions. Talk about how he or she might find answers to those questions.
- Prompt the child to think more. Ask: The planet Uranus looks blue. What gives it this color?

Pogo Books are published by Jump!
5357 Penn Avenue South
Minneapolis, MN 55419
www.jumplibrary.com

Copyright © 2023 Jump!
International copyright reserved in all countries. No part of this book may be reproduced in any form without written permission from the publisher.

Library of Congress Cataloging-in-Publication Data

Names: Schuh, Mari C., 1975- author.
Title: Uranus : the coldest planet / by Mari Schuh.
Description: Minneapolis, MN: Jump!, Inc., [2023]
Series: Our solar system | Includes index.
Audience: Ages 7-10
Identifiers: LCCN 2022032928 (print)
LCCN 2022032929 (ebook)
ISBN 9798885243735 (hardcover)
ISBN 9798885243742 (paperback)
ISBN 9798885243759 (ebook)
Subjects: LCSH: Uranus (Planet)—Juvenile literature.
Classification: LCC QB681 .S38 2023 (print)
LCC QB681 (ebook)
DDC 523.47—dc23/eng20220919
LC record available at https://lccn.loc.gov/2022032928
LC ebook record available at https://lccn.loc.gov/2022032929

Editor: Jenna Gleisner
Designer: Emma Bersie

Photo Credits: StockByM/iStock, cover (Uranus), 18-19 (Uranus); Maliflower73/Shutterstock, cover (background), 18-19 (background); ManuMata/Shutterstock, 1; SciePro/Shutterstock, 3; Pe3k/Shutterstock, 4 (Uranus); ixpert/Shutterstock, 4 (Earth); Byron Moore/Dreamstime, 5; Nerthuz/iStock, 6-7 (Uranus); AstroStar/Shutterstock, 6-7 (background); uranus/Alamy, 8-9; buradaki/Shutterstock, 10-11; NASA/JPL-Caltech, 12, 17tl; Sebastian_Photography/Shutterstock, 13 (Uranus); 7xpert/Dreamstime, 13 (Earth); NASA images/Shutterstock, 14-15 (Uranus); sripfoto/Shutterstock, 14-15 (background); Science Photo Library/Alamy, 16; NASA/JPL, 17tr, 17bl; NASA, 17br; Klanarong Chitmung/Shutterstock, 17 (background); Beyond Space/Shutterstock, 18-19 (Saturn); NASA Hubble, 20-21 (Uranus); olivierlaurentphoto/Shutterstock, 20-21 (Hubble Space Telescope); Andrey Simonenko/Dreamstime, 23.

Printed in the United States of America at Corporate Graphics in North Mankato, Minnesota.

For Paige

rings

Rings circle this big planet. The inner rings are dark and thin. The outer rings are bright. They are easier to see.

Uranus has a thick **atmosphere**. It is made of different gases. Methane is a gas. It gives the planet a blue-green color.

DID YOU KNOW?

Scientists think it might rain diamonds inside Uranus! How? **Pressure** deep inside the planet is strong. It might turn tiny pieces of **matter** into diamonds.

All planets **orbit** the Sun. One full orbit around the Sun is one year. One Earth year is 365 days. Uranus is far from the Sun. It has a long way to travel. One orbit, or year, on Uranus is 84 Earth years!

TAKE A LOOK!

Uranus is the seventh planet from the Sun. Take a look!

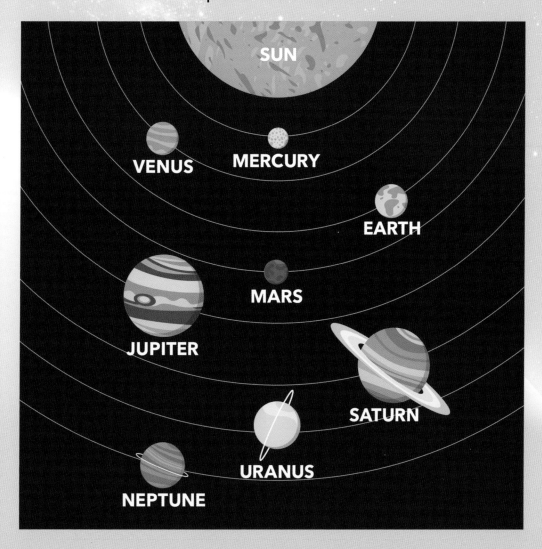

SUN

VENUS

MERCURY

EARTH

MARS

JUPITER

SATURN

URANUS

NEPTUNE

axis

All planets spin. One full spin is one day. One spin, or day, on Uranus takes 17 hours.

Uranus's **axis** is tilted, so it has a unique spin. It spins on its side! Scientists think a large body twice the size of Earth crashed into the planet. This might have caused it to tilt.

DID YOU KNOW?

Every planet has seasons. Seasons on Uranus are long. Each season lasts 21 Earth years!

CHAPTER 2

. . . .

ICE GIANT

Uranus is very cold and windy. It holds the record for the coldest temperature in our solar system. It reached –371 degrees Fahrenheit (–224 degrees Celsius). *Brrr!*

A planet's **gravity** depends on its size, **mass**, and **density**. Gravity on Uranus is similar to gravity on Earth. But the two planets are very different.

For example, we cannot stand on Uranus. Why? It does not have a solid surface. It is made mostly of flowing, icy liquid. That is why this planet is called an ice giant.

TAKE A LOOK!

Uranus has a small, rocky **core**. What are its other layers?
Take a look!

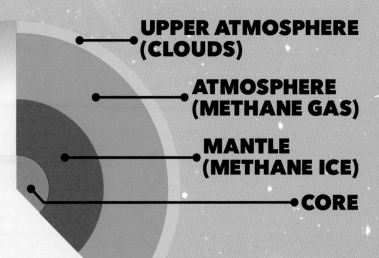

**UPPER ATMOSPHERE
(CLOUDS)**

**ATMOSPHERE
(METHANE GAS)**

**MANTLE
(METHANE ICE)**

CORE

CHAPTER 3

AMAZING DISCOVERIES

Voyager 2 is the only **spacecraft** that has visited Uranus. It traveled near the planet in 1986. It got about 50,000 miles (80,500 kilometers) away from Uranus's clouds. *Voyager 2* measured how fast Uranus spins.

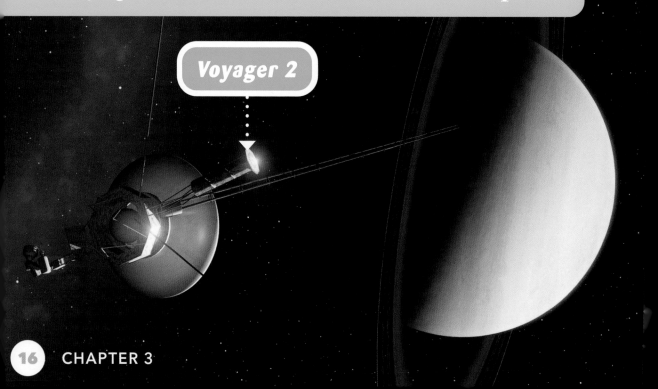

Voyager 2

Miranda

Titania

Oberon

Puck

Voyager 2 discovered two new rings. It also discovered 10 of Uranus's 27 moons. One is named Puck. It is about 90 miles (145 km) wide. Puck travels around Uranus in less than one Earth day.

In 2006, scientists learned more about Uranus. They found out that its outer ring is bright blue. Rings around planets are usually a reddish color. Only Saturn and Uranus have blue outer rings.

Saturn's blue ring

Uranus's blue ring

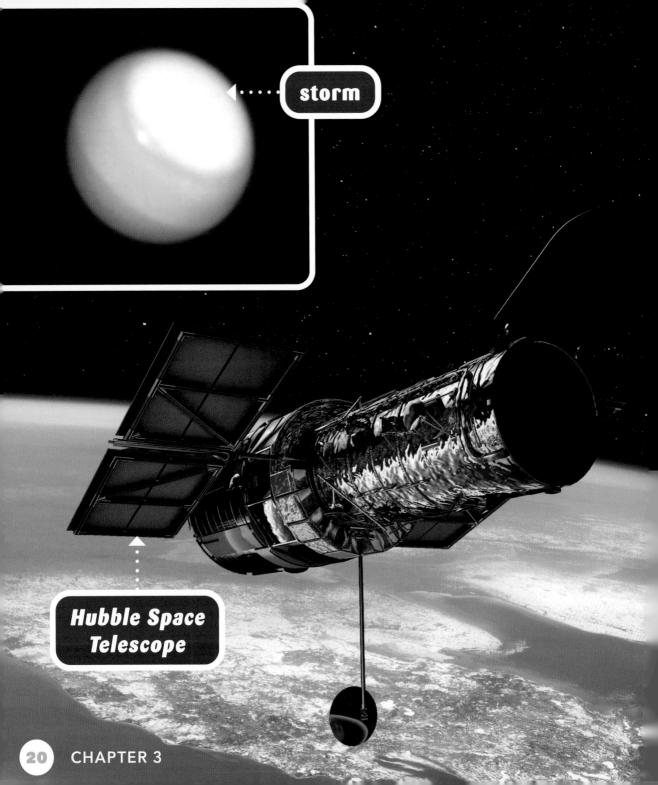

storm

Hubble Space Telescope

Scientists use the *Hubble Space Telescope* to learn about Uranus. In 2018, they saw a huge storm. It was on the planet's north **pole**.

Scientists want to learn more about this planet. What more would you like to learn?

DID YOU KNOW?

Astronomer William Herschel discovered Uranus in 1781.

ACTIVITIES & TOOLS

COMPARE PLANET SIZES

Uranus is the third largest planet in our solar system. See how the sizes of the planets compare in this fun activity!

What You Need:
- 8 round food items of different sizes
- paper
- pen or pencil

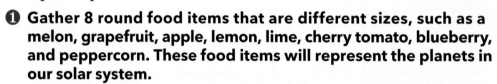

❶ Gather 8 round food items that are different sizes, such as a melon, grapefruit, apple, lemon, lime, cherry tomato, blueberry, and peppercorn. These food items will represent the planets in our solar system.

❷ Look back at the diagram in the book, or have an adult help you research the sizes of the planets. Match each food item with a planet based on size. Write each planet name on a piece of paper. Place each piece of paper next to its planet.

❸ Arrange the foods in order by size. Arrange them big to small.

❹ Study the food and the planets they are matched to. Uranus, Neptune, Saturn, and Jupiter are gas planets. How does their size compare to the other planets, which are solid and rocky?

astronomer: A scientist who studies stars, planets, and space.

atmosphere: The mixture of gases that surrounds a planet.

axis: An imaginary line through the center of an object, around which the object spins.

core: The center, most inner part of a planet.

density: The measure of how heavy or light an object is for its size. Density is measured by dividing an object's mass by its volume.

gravity: The force that pulls things toward the center of a planet and keeps them from floating away.

mass: The amount of physical matter an object has.

matter: Something that has weight and takes up space, such as a solid, liquid, or gas.

orbit: To travel in a circular path around something.

planet: A large body that orbits, or travels in circles around, the Sun.

pole: One of the two geographical points that are farthest from the equator.

pressure: The force produced by pressing on something.

solar system: The Sun, together with its orbiting bodies, such as the planets, their moons, and asteroids, comets, and meteors.

spacecraft: Vehicles that travel in space.

INDEX

TO LEARN MORE

Finding more information is as easy as 1, 2, 3.

❶ Go to www.factsurfer.com

❷ Enter "Uranus" into the search box.

❸ Choose your book to see a list of websites.

FACT
SURFER